## Master KS2 Reading with CGP!

When it comes to reading in Year 3, practice makes perfect. That's why CGP have made this indispensable Question Book!

It's full of fascinating texts by a variety of authors — each with practice questions to check pupils' understanding and deepen their knowledge of techniques used by authors.

We've even included helpful answers at the back of the book.

## What CGP is all about

Our sole aim here at CGP is to produce the highest quality books — carefully written, immaculately presented and dangerously close to being funny.

Then we work our socks off to get them out to you — at the cheapest possible prices.

# Contents

**About this Book** ....................................................................................... 3

**Poems about Trees** ................................................................................. 4
**Poetry** by Edith Nesbit and A. E. Housman

**Small School, Big Changes** ................................................................. 10
**Report** by Susan Hughes

**The Viking Warrior** ............................................................................... 16
**Story in an Everyday Setting** by Maxine Petrie

**Orpheus and Euridice** .......................................................................... 22
**Myth** by Duncan Lindsay

**Build Your Own Solar System** ............................................................. 28
**Instruction Text** by Kjartan Poskitt

**Alice in Wonderland** ............................................................................. 34
**Playscript** by Glyn Maxwell

**Childhood in the 1800s** ........................................................................ 40
**Non-Chronological Report** from the *Oxford Illustrated Dictionary of 19th Century Language*

**The Mystery of Wickworth Manor** ....................................................... 46
**Adventure Story** by Elen Caldecott

**Danny, the Champion of the World** .................................................... 52
**Children's Fiction** by Roald Dahl

**Answers** ................................................................................................ 58

**National Curriculum Content Areas** ................................................... 64

---

Published by CGP

Anthologist: Christopher Edge
Questions written by Amanda MacNaughton
Consultant: Julie Docker
Reviewers: Sam Bensted, Juliette Green, Maxine Petrie
Editors: Melissa Gardner, Kelsey Hammond, Christopher Lindle,
         Sam Norman, Rosa Roberts

With thanks to Izzy Bowen, Alison Griffin and Holly Robinson for the proofreading.
With thanks to Ana Pungartnik for the copyright research.

ISBN: 978 1 78908 356 9
Printed by Elanders Ltd, Newcastle upon Tyne.

Text, design, layout and original illustrations
© Coordination Group Publications Ltd. (CGP) 2019
All rights reserved.

---

Photocopying this book is not permitted, even if you have a CLA licence.
Extra copies are available from CGP with next day delivery • 0800 1712 712 • www.cgpbooks.co.uk

# About this Book

This book consists of nine stimulating texts for pupils to read, with two sets of questions for each text:
- Question Set 1 checks that pupils understand the text as a whole, with lots of retrieval questions.
- Question Set 2 gets pupils thinking more deeply, with more questions requiring inference.

## Question Pages

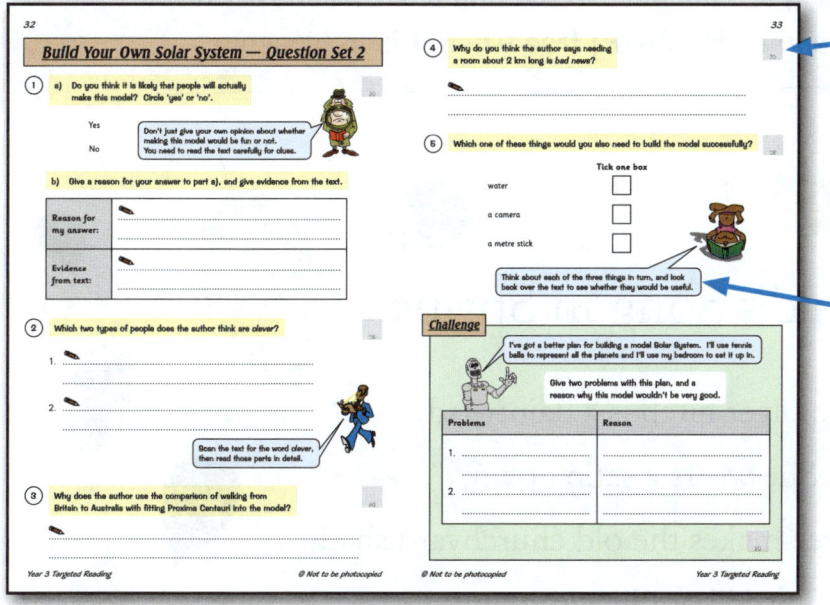

The mark boxes give the national curriculum content area for the question:

Pupils are given tips on how to tackle some questions.

The recurring characters familiarise pupils with different types of question:

Scanning the text    Finding evidence in the text

## National Curriculum References

Here is a key to the national curriculum references for the different question types:

| | |
|---|---|
| 2A | give / explain the meaning of words in context |
| 2B | retrieve and record information / identify key details from fiction and non-fiction |
| 2C | summarise main ideas from more than one paragraph |
| 2D | make inferences from the text / explain and justify inferences with evidence from the text |
| 2E | predict what might happen from details stated and implied |
| 2F | identify / explain how information / narrative content is related and contributes to meaning as a whole |
| 2G | identify / explain how meaning is enhanced through choice of words and phrases |
| 2H | make comparisons within the text |

At the back of the book, you'll find a table where you can record the pupil's performance in the different content areas:

# Text 1 — Poetry

## Poems about Trees

Start reading here. There might be important information in the introduction.

In these two poems, the poets talk about their favourite trees. Edith Nesbit, in her poem 'Child's Song in Spring', describes different types of trees as if they are people. In his poem 'Loveliest of trees', A. E. Housman talks about the cherry tree when it is in blossom.

### Child's Song in Spring

The silver birch is a dainty lady,
She wears a satin gown;
The elm tree makes the old churchyard shady,
She will not live in town.

The English oak is a sturdy fellow,
He gets his green coat late;
The willow is smart in a suit of yellow,
While brown the beech trees wait.

The chestnut's proud and the lilac's pretty,
The poplar's gentle and tall,
But the plane tree's kind to the poor dull city —
I love him best of all!

by Edith Nesbit

# Loveliest of trees

Loveliest of trees, the cherry now
Is hung with bloom along the bough,
And stands about the woodland ride
Wearing white for Eastertide.

      Now, of my threescore years and ten,
      Twenty will not come again,
      And take from seventy springs a score,
      It only leaves me fifty more.

And since to look at things in bloom
Fifty springs are little room,
About the woodlands I will go
To see the cherry hung with snow.

by A. E. Housman

### Glossary
bough — branch of a tree
Eastertide — the season coming after Easter
threescore years and ten — seventy years (how long people expected they would live)
score — twenty

## Consider
Think of one thing the two poems have in common, and one thing that is different between them.

# Poems About Trees — Question Set 1

**1** Using the poem 'Child's Song in Spring' to help you, draw lines to match each tree to its colour.

| willow | | brown |
| --- | --- | --- |
| birch | | silver |
| beech | | yellow |

**2** Which of the following pairs of words from the poem 'Child's Song in Spring' are opposite in meaning?

**Tick one box**

old and dull ☐

dainty and sturdy ☐

smart and proud ☐

gentle and kind ☐

> It can help to identify which words are definitely <u>not</u> opposites first.

**3** The poem 'Child's Song in Spring' describes nine different trees. Write down the names of four of these but make sure they aren't mentioned in Question 1.

1. ....................................................................................
2. ....................................................................................
3. ....................................................................................
4. ....................................................................................

④ **In the second poem, where will the poet go to find cherry trees in blossom?**

✏️ ..................................................................................................................

⑤ **a) What colour are the flowers on the cherry tree?**

✏️ ..................................................................................................................

**b) Copy a line in the poem which tells us its colour.**

✏️ ..................................................................................................................

> Unfortunately, the text doesn't say 'the flowers are blue' or 'the flowers are red'. You have to dig beneath the surface to find the answer.

⑥ **Complete the sentences below using information from both poems.**

Edith Nesbit's favourite tree is ............................................. .

The poem ............................................. is about one tree.

The tree that makes the churchyard shady is the ............................................. .

............................................. thinks he will live for 70 years.

> When you think you've got the right answer, read the whole sentence again to make sure your answer makes sense.

# Poems About Trees — Question Set 2

**1** Satin is a glossy material. Edith Nesbit describes the silver birch as wearing *a satin gown*. What do you think she is telling you about the tree?

..................................................................................................................................

**2** Complete the table below to show which poem each rhyming pattern matches.

| Rhyming pattern: | Name of the poem it is used in: |
|---|---|
| AABB | .................................................................. |
| ABAB | .................................................................. |

> Underline the words at the end of each line in the poems.
> '**AABB**' means line 1 and 2 rhyme, and lines 3 and 4 rhyme.
> '**ABAB**' means lines 1 and 3 rhyme, and lines 2 and 4 rhyme.

**3** How old was the poet when he wrote 'Loveliest of trees'?

**Tick one box**

20 ☐

50 ☐

70 ☐

> The poet describes his age in terms of how many seasons of spring he has seen.

**4)** Why do you think Edith Nesbit thinks the plane tree is *kind to the poor dull city?*

..................................................................................................................

..................................................................................................................

**5)** a) 'Child's Song in Spring' is full of metaphors. Tick all the phrases below which are metaphors.

Tick all that apply

The silver birch is a dainty lady. ☐

The willow is smart in a suit of yellow. ☐

The lilac's pretty. ☐

The English oak is a sturdy fellow. ☐

> A metaphor is when something is described as something it's not.

b) Find and copy a metaphor from 'Loveliest of trees'.

..................................................................................................................

## Challenge

> The poem has it all wrong! Cherry trees don't usually have snow on them in springtime.

**Explain to the cat what the poet really means in the last line of 'Loveliest of trees'.**

..................................................................................................................

..................................................................................................................

..................................................................................................................

## Text 2 — Report

### Small School, Big Changes

Reports are a type of non-fiction text that provide readers with information on a subject or topic. The following report is about a small school in Iran, which became known as the smallest school in the world.

# Small School, Big Changes

The remote fishing village of Kalou, near the Persian Gulf in Iran, is so small that it doesn't appear on satellite maps of the Earth. Its school has just four students. But thanks to a blog about the village and its tiny school, life changed almost overnight for kids in Kalou, especially the girls.

Kalou didn't even have a school before 2008, when a teacher named Abdul-Muhammad She'rani arrived with the goal of setting one up. The village let him use a fishing shed, and on the first day of school, he and the students cleaned it out and set up a classroom inside.

### Putting Kalou on the Map

Abdul-Muhammad was so excited about the new school, called Shahid Rajaei, that he started a blog about it. He described the students' enthusiasm, as well as the limited supplies and space he had to work with. In one entry, he called his school the smallest in Iran. News channels picked up the story of his tiny school and it caught the attention of people all over the world. UNESCO named it "the World's Smallest School".

People began sending letters, money, textbooks and other gifts. Someone paid for the village to build a brand new schoolhouse. The government sent new desks and a computer. Almost overnight, the kids in Kalou had gone from having no school to having one of the most famous schools in the world.

**Fact:**
UNICEF estimates that around the world more girls than boys are missing out on school. How many girls is that? About 60 million.

Shahid Rajaei Elementary School

## Changing Minds & Lives

All this attention had a big effect on the life of the school's oldest female student, Hamideh. After finishing at Shahid Rajaei in 2009, Hamideh started going to secondary school in a city 40 kilometres away. That would have been unthinkable just a few years earlier.

Hamideh's father had not planned for Hamideh to continue her education past primary school. Most parents in the village thought that girls did not need to go further in school. They also did not want their daughters moving to the city, which was the only option if they wanted to continue their studies.

Abdul-Muhammad says, "It was our tiny school and the many visitors it drew to Kalou that made Hamideh's father change his mind. Since the school got famous worldwide, he realised that Hamideh would benefit from continuing her education. Hamideh was breaking tradition to do so."

Once Hamideh's father agreed, Abdul-Muhammad convinced the government to set up a school bus route to drive Hamideh to secondary school and back every day. That way, she didn't have to move to the city. And now that the village has a school bus stop, younger girls will be able to continue their education when they finish at Shahid Rajaei – just like Hamideh!

An extract from *My School, Our World* by Susan Hughes.

**Glossary**

blog — a website which is like an online diary

UNESCO — an organisation which supports education (the United Nations Educational, Scientific and Cultural Organisation)

UNICEF — a charity which helps children (the United Nations Children's Fund)

**Consider**
What does someone like Abdul-Muhammad have to be like to achieve what he has achieved? Do you know anyone who has made a real difference to your local community?

# Small School, Big Changes — Question Set 1

**1** Why doesn't the village of Kalou appear on satellite maps of the Earth?

..................................................................................................

**2** What did Abdul-Muhammad She'rani want to do when he arrived in the village?

**Tick one box**

He wanted the village to be famous. ☐

He wanted to set up a fishing business. ☐

He wanted to set up the first school. ☐

He wanted to write a blog. ☐

**3** Draw lines to match the name on the left with its description on the right. One has been done for you.

| Shahid Rajaei | | A student of the school in Kalou. |
| Hamideh | | The teacher who changed the lives of children in Kalou. |
| Kalou | | An international group set up to support children's education. |
| Abdul-Muhammad She'rani | | A tiny fishing village in Iran. |
| UNICEF | | The name of the first school in Kalou. |

(Kalou is matched to "An international group set up to support children's education.")

With these matching questions, do the ones you feel sure about first.

Who? What? Where? When? Why?

**4** Find and copy one phrase from the text which tells us that the story of this tiny school became known in many other countries.

..................................................................................................................

..................................................................................................................

*The question says 'Find and copy one phrase...'. This means you need to find <u>a few words</u> in the text, and write them out <u>carefully</u> as your answer.*

**5** Name three things the school was sent from people who wanted to help.

1. ..................................................................................................................

2. ..................................................................................................................

3. ..................................................................................................................

**6** Which of the following statements best summarises the section called *Changing Minds and Lives*?

**Tick one box**

It is about a girl and her father who argue whether she should go to school or not. ☐

It is about a girl called Hamideh who goes on to become a secondary school teacher. ☐

It is about a girl who has to move away from home to be able to go to secondary school. ☐

It is about a girl whose father changes his mind about her education. ☐

*'Summarising' means giving the main idea without too much detail.*

© Not to be photocopied

Year 3 Targeted Reading

# Small School, Big Changes — Question Set 2

**1** Why do you think the author chose *Putting Kalou on the Map* as a heading for the second section of this report?

..................................................................................
..................................................................................
..................................................................................

> Think about how famous Kalou was <u>before</u> and <u>after</u> the school was set up.

**2** How do you think Abdul-Muhammad She'rani felt when he started receiving gifts and money for the school? Why do you think this?

..................................................................................
..................................................................................
..................................................................................

**3** Why did Hamideh's father change his mind about Hamideh going to secondary school?

..................................................................................
..................................................................................
..................................................................................

**4** How do you know from the teacher's blog that the children who attended this school were happy?

..................................................................................
..................................................................................

> Use evidence from the text in your answer.

**5** a) Read the fact from UNICEF. Which one of the following words do you think the author wants you to feel when reading this?

shocked ☐    happy ☐

scared ☐    bored ☐

b) Why do you think she wants you to feel like this?

✏️
................................................................................................................
................................................................................................................
................................................................................................................
................................................................................................................

## Challenge

This amazing little school changed the life of the boys in Kalou more than the girls.

Do you agree or disagree? Explain your answer using evidence from the text to support your own opinion.

................................................................................................................
................................................................................................................
................................................................................................................
................................................................................................................
................................................................................................................

# Text 3 — Story in an Everyday Setting

## The Viking Warrior

Story writing often takes us into the mind of its main character. In this story extract, a boy called Tristan is surprised to be given a job to do by his teacher.

Tristan had never liked school. From the moment he was dragged kicking and screaming by his mum into the Reception class three years ago, he had detested every single second that he spent at Summertown Academy. This had not endeared him to the teachers or children, and his stony face hid a simmering cauldron of anger at being forced to be there. He did not realise that this made the other children avoid him, and although he pretended that he did not care, he often looked longingly at pairs or groups of children playing happily together.

His cousin Rosie was home-educated, and she went on lots of fun trips to museums and castles with Auntie Jenny, and she didn't have to wear a horrid, scratchy school uniform or get up early for school. When Tristan had asked his mum about being educated at home, she had snapped that as a single parent, she had to go out to work. Tristan changed the subject as he knew his mum felt bad about him having to go to breakfast club and after school club. Tristan hated these clubs almost as much as he disliked school, but at least he got to play with the set of Formula One cars.

The black sky seemed to echo Tristan's mood as he sat on the carpet gazing out of the window on the first day of the new school year. Miss Benson was droning on about good behaviour, high expectations, neat work blah blah blah, and Tristan had stopped listening until her heard her say,

"... and our new topic this term is the Vikings." There was nothing that Tristan didn't know about the Vikings. He had read books and books on the subject, and when alone in the playground, he had often imagined himself as a Viking warrior, swinging his sword around his head and bellowing at the children to stop being so irritating.

"We also have a new boy today. His name is Ayrton," continued Miss Benson. All eyes swivelled to a small, dark-haired boy, sitting grinning at the back of the class, fidgeting restlessly. "Tristan, can you look after Ayrton and make him feel welcome?" asked his crazy teacher. Did she really expect Tristan to be a role model? He could tell that his classmates were equally surprised that Miss Benson had chosen Tristan to help Ayrton settle in.

As they sat at their desks, Ayrton leaned over to Tristan, whispering, "She's a bossy teacher, isn't she? I'm Ayrton. My dad named me that after a racing driver from years and years ago. I love the Vikings, don't you? Perhaps this school won't be as boring as my last one." Unused to anyone talking to him, Tristan stared wide-eyed at his new-found friend. Maybe, just maybe, school might not be such a nightmare after all...

**Written by Maxine Petrie**

## Consider

In the text, it says that Tristan *often looked longingly at pairs or groups of children playing happily together.* What do you think this tells us about him?

# The Viking Warrior — Question Set 1

**1** For how long had Tristan not enjoyed school?

..................................................................................................................

*This question is asking 'for how long' — this means you're looking for a length of time.*

Who? What? Where? When? Why?

**2** Use the text to decide if the following statements are true or false.

|  | True | False |
|---|---|---|
| The children in Tristan's class do not like him. | ☐ | ☐ |
| Tristan lives with his mum and dad. | ☐ | ☐ |
| Tristan has a cousin called Jenny. | ☐ | ☐ |
| Tristan likes playing with cars. | ☐ | ☐ |

**3** Give two reasons (other than he doesn't like school) why Tristan wants to be home-schooled like his cousin.

1. ..................................................................................................................
..................................................................................................................

2. ..................................................................................................................
..................................................................................................................

*Scan the text for the part where it talks about his cousin, then look carefully for the answers.*

Year 3 Targeted Reading © Not to be photocopied

**4** Match the words from the text (on the left) with the correct meaning (on the right).

| detested | said angrily |
| snapped | turned around |
| droning | hated |
| swivelled | speaking boringly |

*Don't rush questions like this. Read all of the words, and match up the ones you're most sure of first.*

**5** a) What does the author compare Tristan's mood to in the classroom?

..................................................................................

b) Which word shows she is comparing Tristan's mood with something else?

..................................................................................

**6** How did Ayrton get his name?

..................................................................................
..................................................................................

# The Viking Warrior — Question Set 2

**1** Find and copy two phrases that show Tristan was not popular with the other children in his class.

1. ...................................................................................................

2. ...................................................................................................

**2** Why do you think the author has used the words *a simmering cauldron of anger* to describe Tristan's feelings about being at school?

...................................................................................................

...................................................................................................

...................................................................................................

> Think about what the words *simmering* and *cauldron* mean. If you don't know, try looking them up in a dictionary.

**3** Why does Tristan start listening to his teacher again?

**Tick one box**

because she says it is play time ☐

because she says Tristan's name ☐

because she says they will be learning about Vikings ☐

because she introduces the new boy, Ayrton ☐

④ **Why were the children *equally surprised* that Miss Benson had chosen Tristan to help Ayrton settle in?**

..................................................................................................................

..................................................................................................................

..................................................................................................................

> Think what you've learned about Tristan throughout the whole text.

⑤ a) **Do you think Tristan and Ayrton will become friends?**

       Yes           No

b) **What makes you think this? Use evidence from the text to support your answer.**

..................................................................................................................

..................................................................................................................

..................................................................................................................

..................................................................................................................

## Challenge

> Tristan really loves his school and has lots of fun there!
>
> Do you agree or disagree? Give reasons to support your answer.

| What I think: | .................................................... |
|---|---|
| Evidence from the text: | .................................................... .................................................... .................................................... .................................................... |

# Text 4 — Myth

# Orpheus and Euridice

Remember to read the introduction. It might contain important information.

Myths are traditional stories told by different cultures. The ancient Greeks believed in different gods and goddesses, such as Hades who was the god of death. In the following story, Hades makes a deal with the musician Orpheus to allow him to bring his wife Euridice back from the underworld...

"What do I do? Euridice would know what to do..."

Orpheus stared up at the monster in front of him. It was Cerberus, Hades' enormous three-headed dog. Each head snapped and snarled at Orpheus, and he was terrified. Euridice had always given him confidence. Without her by his side, he was full of fear and doubt. But if he ever wanted to see her again, he had to save her from the underworld.

Thinking of Euridice calmed him down, and suddenly, Orpheus got an idea. He began to play a lullaby on his harp, and sang to the monster.

"Go to sleep. Go to sleep. Go to sleep giant doggy."

Cerberus was powerless against the song. As Orpheus played and sang, one by one, each of the dog's three massive heads fell into a deep sleep.

"Beautiful! Very well done," came a voice from the darkness. It was Hades, who clapped his hands as he approached Orpheus. "What do you want from me?" he asked Orpheus.

"Please," begged Orpheus. "My wife Euridice is here. Let me take her with me and bring her back to life. I don't know how to live without her."

Hades frowned at Orpheus. "I don't just let people come back to life willy-nilly you know," he grumbled. "However, your music impressed me. How about I make you a deal?"

"You may walk out of the underworld back to the land of the living, and Euridice will follow behind you. But you must not look back to check that she is following. If you look behind you, even once, before you have left the underworld, Euridice will stay here forever."

"I'll do it," agreed Orpheus.

"Start walking then," replied Hades. Orpheus turned and began to walk back the way he had come, towards the land of the living.

"Orpheus?" came a voice from behind him.

"Euridice!" cried Orpheus. It was his wife's voice. All he wanted to do was to turn around and see her once again. But he remembered his deal with Hades, and he kept looking ahead. "Just follow me."

So Orpheus walked on through the underworld, happy that his wife was with him again. But as he got closer to the exit, he began to worry. How could he be sure Euridice was following him? What if she'd got lost?

"Euridice?" he called out. "I'm here!" replied Euridice.

So Orpheus kept walking, but he kept worrying. He'd only heard her voice. How could he be sure she was really there? Maybe Hades was playing a trick on him. He was just a few steps from the exit, but he couldn't stop himself. He turned around.

"Orpheus… No…" Euridice gasped. There she was, following his every step. But Orpheus had not trusted her. He'd let his doubts take over. He watched in horror as Euridice was pulled back into the underworld. And she'd stay there forever.

Written by Duncan Lindsay

## Discuss

If Orpheus returned to the underworld at the end of the story, what would the conversation be like between him and Hades? Discuss your ideas with a partner.

# Orpheus and Euridice — Question Set 1

**1** What makes Cerberus such an unusual dog?

✏️ ..............................................................................................

**2** Why does Orpheus miss Euridice so much?

**Tick one box**

She loved dogs. ☐

She could play the harp. ☐

She gave him confidence. ☐

She was a good singer. ☐

**3** How did thinking of his wife help Orpheus to deal with Cerberus even though she wasn't there?

✏️ ..............................................................................................
..............................................................................................

> Don't just guess at the answer. Go back to the text and see what it tells you before Orpheus has his idea.

**4** Which word on the first page shows that Cerberus couldn't control himself when Orpheus played and sang?

✏️ ..............................................................................................

**5** Draw lines to match the name of the character in the story (on the left) with the most suitable description (on the right).

| Hades    |          | musician         |
| Orpheus  |          | three-headed dog |
| Euridice |          | god of death     |
| Cerberus |          | wife of Orpheus  |

*With matching questions, do the ones you are sure of first.*

Who? What? Where? When? Why?

**6** Number these events in the order they happen in the text. The first one has been done for you.

Orpheus knows Euridice is walking behind him. ☐

Orpheus loses faith and goes back on his promise. ☐

Orpheus walks away from the underworld. ☐

Orpheus and Hades strike a deal. 1

*When you have to number events, it's like finding a secret 4-digit code. First <u>find</u> and <u>underline</u> each of the events in the text. Then <u>number</u> the events in the text in the order they appear. Finally, <u>match</u> the events in the question to the numbers in the text.*

# Orpheus and Euridice — Question Set 2

**1** Who is Orpheus speaking to when he says *What do I do? Euridice would know what to do...*?

- Hades ☐
- himself ☐
- Cerberus ☐
- Euridice ☐

> For this question, you need to picture the scene, and put yourself in the place of Orpheus.

**2** Find and copy two pieces of evidence that show Hades is pleased with how Orpheus has handled Cerberus.

1. .......................................................................................................
   .......................................................................................................

2. .......................................................................................................
   .......................................................................................................

> When the question says 'Find and copy', you need to copy the words from the text <u>carefully</u>.

**3** Which of the following words show Hades is not keen to let Orpheus have his wife back? Tick two words.

- frowned ☐
- deal ☐
- impressed ☐
- grumbled ☐

Year 3 Targeted Reading

**4** How could he be sure Euridice was following him? What if she'd got lost? What do these questions show about how Orpheus is feeling?

✏️
..................................................................................................................................
..................................................................................................................................

**5** a) In the final paragraph, what one word apart from 'No' shows how Euridice feels about Orpheus turning around?

✏️
..................................................................................................................................

b) How do you think she must feel? Give a reason for your answer.

| How Euridice must feel: | .................................................................................. |
|---|---|
| Why I think this: | .................................................................................. |

## Challenge

*I don't understand. Why did Hades not want him to turn around?*

Explain to the monkey why Hades told Orpheus not to turn around.

..................................................................................................................................
..................................................................................................................................
..................................................................................................................................
..................................................................................................................................

# Text 5 — Instruction Text

## Build Your Own Solar System

Instruction texts tell readers how to do something. The following instruction text is from a book called *The Gobsmacking Galaxy* by Kjartan Poskitt. This section tells readers how they could make their own scale model of our solar system.

To get an idea of how big our galaxy is, you first need to understand how big our solar system is. The best way of doing that is to build a model of it. Here's the bad news — you are going to need a room about 2 km long! (If you are clever enough to understand this sort of thing, the scale of this model is going to be about 1:2,500,000.)

### Here's what you will need:

- Two ball bearings (tiny metal balls used in machines)
- Two peas
- A snooker ball
- A tennis ball
- Two golf balls
- A pinhead
- Some sand
- A washing machine

### What you do:

1. Paint the washing machine yellow and put it at one end of the room. This is the **SUN**.
2. 23 metres away from the SUN put down one of your ball bearings. This is **MERCURY**.
3. Keep going another 20 metres and then put down a pea. This is **VENUS**.
4. After a further 17 metres put down the other pea. This is **EARTH**. If you want to show the **MOON**, put the pinhead down about 15 centimetres from the Earth.
5. 31 metres further along, put down the other ball bearing. This is **MARS**.

6. You now have to walk another 220 metres, but when you get about half way sprinkle some sand about. This is the **ASTEROID BELT**.

7. Once you have completed your 220 metre walk you can put down the tennis ball, which is **JUPITER**.

8. 260 metres later you can put down the snooker ball to represent **SATURN**.

9. Keep going for 577 metres... then put down a golf ball. This is **URANUS**.

10. You'll have to go another 651 metres before you can put down the second golf ball, and this is **NEPTUNE**.

There! You have made a rough scale model of the Solar System with everything approximately the right size. Don't the planets look tiny in all that empty space? It makes you realise how clever scientists must be to send rockets out to visit them, and don't forget, the planets are not in a nice straight line but they all move round all the time!

So much for our planets, but just suppose we wanted to show the nearest star to our sun on this model?

The star that comes nearest to us is called Proxima Centauri. Guess how far you would have to walk to fit in with the rest of your Solar System model?

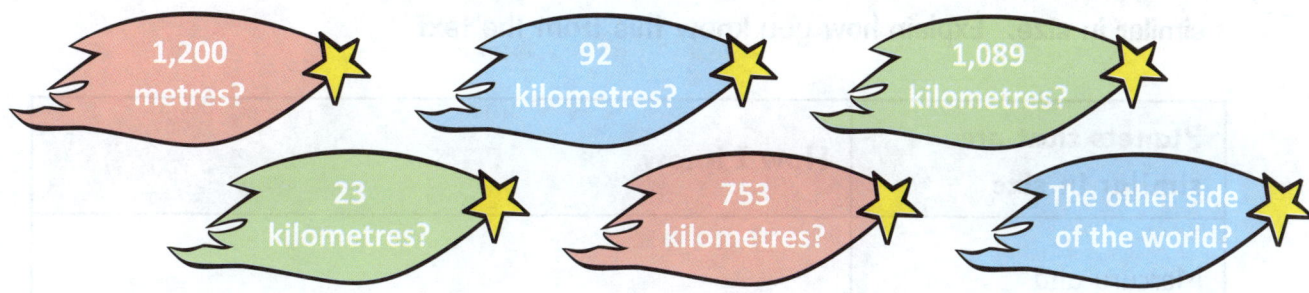

1,200 metres?    92 kilometres?    1,089 kilometres?    23 kilometres?    753 kilometres?    The other side of the world?

In fact, you would need to walk 16,856 kilometres to fit Proxima Centauri onto the model... about the same distance as from Britain to Australia!

An adapted extract from *The Gobsmacking Galaxy* by Kjartan Poskitt.

## Consider

Imagine you could interview one of the scientists who has sent rockets into space. What questions would you ask them about the size of the Solar System?

# Build Your Own Solar System — Question Set 1

**1** Why does the text suggest building a model of the Solar System?

......................................................................................................................

**2** Draw lines to match the feature of the Solar System on the left with the object used to represent it in the model.

| Sun | | sand |
| --- | --- | --- |
| Venus | | ball bearing |
| Asteroid Belt | | washing machine |
| Mars | | pea |
| Moon | | pinhead |

Scan the text for each of the things on the left to help you find the answers.

**3** Complete the table to show which three pairs of planets are similar in size. Explain how you know this from the text.

| Planets that are similar in size | How I know |
| --- | --- |
| Mercury and .............................. | .............................................. |
| Venus and .............................. | .............................................. |
| Uranus and .............................. | .............................................. |

Year 3 Targeted Reading © Not to be photocopied

**4** Number these planets according to how close they are to the Sun. Start with the closest. The first one has been done for you.

Jupiter ☐

Venus ☐

Mercury [1]

Uranus ☐

Earth ☐

> Time to find the secret code to unlock the text! First <u>find</u> each of these five planets in the text and <u>underline</u> them. Then <u>number</u> the planets in the text in the order they appear. Then <u>match</u> the planets in the question with the numbers you've written on your text.

**5** Circle the word or phrase below which could replace the word *approximately* in the text.

different from          similar to          smaller than

bigger than          exactly

**6** Copy a word from the text that means how big things are in the model compared to real life.

..................................................................................................

> The question asks for 'a word' — so your answer should just be <u>one word</u> that appears in the text.

# Build Your Own Solar System — Question Set 2

**1**    a)   Do you think it is likely that people will actually make this model? Circle 'yes' or 'no'.

       Yes

       No

*Don't just give your own opinion about whether making this model would be fun or not. You need to read the text carefully for clues.*

   b)   Give a reason for your answer to part a), and give evidence from the text.

| Reason for my answer: | ................................................................................................................ |
|---|---|
| Evidence from text: | ................................................................................................................ |

**2**    Which two types of people does the author think are *clever*?

1. ..........................................................................................................

2. ..........................................................................................................

*Scan the text for the word clever, then read those parts in detail.*

**3**    Why does the author use the comparison of walking from Britain to Australia with fitting Proxima Centauri into the model?

..........................................................................................................

..........................................................................................................

Year 3 Targeted Reading

**4** Why do you think the author says needing a room about 2 km long is *bad news*?

✏️ ..................................................................................................

..................................................................................................

**5** Which one of these things would you also need to build the model successfully?

**Tick one box**

water ☐

a camera ☐

a metre stick ☐

Think about each of the three things in turn, and look back over the text to see whether they would be useful.

## Challenge

I've got a better plan for building a model Solar System. I'll use tennis balls to represent all the planets and I'll use my bedroom to set it up in.

Give two problems with this plan, and a reason why this model wouldn't be very good.

| Problems | Reason |
|---|---|
| 1. .............................................. .............................................. | .............................................. .............................................. |
| 2. .............................................. .............................................. | .............................................. .............................................. |

# Text 6 — Playscript

## Alice in Wonderland

In this play adaptation of Lewis Carroll's novel *Alice in Wonderland*, Alice has followed a white rabbit and fallen into Wonderland. At first she thinks this must be the new school which she is about to start in the real world.

*A strange gate appears and opens.*

ALICE: Curiouser and curiouser… It must be – it must be *tomorrow*, this must be boring-school! But it's really not *that* boring…

*The* WHITE RABBIT *runs through.*

ALICE: White Rabbit!

W RABBIT: Oh dear, oh dear, I shall be late, I shall be late!

ALICE: Stop, White Rabbit, stop, I need to ask you something, I'm a new girl!

W RABBIT: No time, no time! Oh my ears and whiskers, how late it's getting, how late!

ALICE: It isn't late it's early! *I'm* early, look!

W RABBIT: What's that? You can't be early when it's late!

ALICE: Oh but I am, I came early, to make a good impression.

W RABBIT: A good impression of what?

ALICE: I said — a new girl.

W RABBIT: May I see your impression of a new girl?

ALICE: Pardon? I don't understand. I'm looking for my classroom.

| | |
|---|---|
| W RABBIT: | Hmm yes that's very good, bravo! Very convincing. |
| ALICE: | Oh. Thank you, well, my mummy said I should make a good impression by being early. So it's not late at all and you shouldn't be so worried. |
| W RABBIT: | But the Queen, the Queen, I'm keeping her waiting! |

*The WHITE RABBIT hurries away.*

| | |
|---|---|
| ALICE: | The *Queen* goes to this school? Well Mary said it was a smart school. Was that yesterday? I — don't remember travelling here, there must have been a train, and look at me — I don't have the black uniform. Oh no! I'll stand out! I'll be the only one! What if the Bully comes, I need to hide, I need to hide! Too late! |

*LIVE FLOWERS come, TIGER-LILY, VIOLET and ROSE, colourful but nonetheless in black uniform. They see ALICE in her blue dress.*

| | |
|---|---|
| TIGER-LILY: | Ha, look at *her*, she hasn't got her uniform. |
| VIOLET: | Yeah look at *her*, standing out like that. |
| ROSE: | *And* she's the only one! |
| ALICE: | I'm new! I'm the new girl! |
| TIGER-LILY: | If she had the right clothes she would fit in very well. |
| VIOLET: | If she had the right look she would look just right. |
| ROSE: | If she was like one of us she'd be just like one of us! |

**An extract from *Alice in Wonderland* adapted by Glyn Maxwell.**

## Discuss

The story of *Alice in Wonderland* takes place in a dream world. Can you find any <u>clues</u> in the text that Alice is in a dream in this extract? Discuss your ideas with a partner.

# Alice in Wonderland — Question Set 1

**1** Where does Alice think she is at first?

..................................................................................................

**2** Which one of these words could replace the word *curiouser*?

Tick one box

sadder ☐

speedier ☐

stranger ☐

curvier ☐

*Curiouser* isn't a real word. You should be able to figure out what Alice means though.

**3** Complete the sentences below so they are correct.
Use either 'early' or 'late' in each gap.

Alice thinks she is ........................................... .

White Rabbit thinks he is ........................................... .

**4** Playscripts have some special layout features compared to other texts.
Draw arrows to match the features in the boxes to the examples in the extract.

| stage direction | name of character speaking | what the character says |

*A strange gate appears and opens.*

ALICE: Curiouser and curiouser... It must be – it must be *tomorrow*, this must be boring-school! But it's really not *that* boring...

*The WHITE RABBIT runs through.*

**5** Use the text to decide if the following statements are true or false.

|  | True | False |
|---|---|---|
| Alice's mummy said she should make a good first impression. | ☐ | ☐ |
| White Rabbit arrived on a train. | ☐ | ☐ |
| The flowers are wearing colourful uniforms. | ☐ | ☐ |
| Alice knows she is in Wonderland. | ☐ | ☐ |

> Scan the text for key words from each statement to help find the answer.

**6** Number these events from 1-4 in the order they happen in the text. The first one has been done for you.

|  | |
|---|---|
| White Rabbit continues on his journey to meet the Queen. | ☐ |
| Alice meets White Rabbit for the first time. | 1 |
| The flowers laugh at Alice's lack of uniform. | ☐ |
| Alice tells White Rabbit that she is a new girl. | ☐ |

> Time to find the secret code! <u>Find</u> and <u>underline</u> each event in the text. <u>Number</u> the underlined events in the order they appear in the text. Finally, <u>match</u> the events in the question to the numbered events in the text.

# Alice in Wonderland — Question Set 2

**1** Why does White Rabbit not have time to stop and talk to Alice?

..................................................................................................................

**2** Which words in the text show that White Rabbit thinks Alice is doing a good job of pretending to be a new girl?

**Tick all that apply**

impression ☐

bravo ☐

convincing ☐

new ☐

*You'll need to read this part of the text again. If you don't know any of the words, try to work out what they mean from the context.*

**3 a)** Which of the following words best describes how Alice is feeling in this extract? Circle the one you've chosen.

excited          happy          confused          angry

*These words aren't in the text. You need to work out what Alice is feeling by what she says.*

**b)** Find and copy two words or phrases which support your answer in part a).

1. ..............................................................................................................

2. ..............................................................................................................

**4** Find and copy two words or phrases to show that White Rabbit is worried about being late.

1. ......................................................................................................

2. ......................................................................................................

Think about which phrases show how the rabbit <u>feels</u> about being late.

**5** Circle the word below which best describes the Live Flowers' behaviour towards Alice. Explain why you think this.

friendly            unfriendly

Why I think this: ..........................................................................

..................................................................................................

..................................................................................................

## Challenge

Stories set in dream worlds often include characters speaking nonsense. Find and copy two parts of the text where a character says something that is confusing or does not make sense.

1. ..........................................................................................

..........................................................................................

2. ..........................................................................................

..........................................................................................

# Text 7 — Non-Chronological Report

## Childhood in the 1800s

Remember to read the introduction. It might contain important information.

Non-chronological reports provide lots of interesting facts about a topic. The text below tells its readers all sorts of things about what life was like for rich and poor children in England in the 19th century.

## Children at Work

The life of a poor child in the 1800s was a harsh one. Children as young as four years old worked 12-hour shifts in factories and mills, down mines, and on the streets as road sweepers and chimney sweeps.

It was a dangerous, terrifying and unhealthy life. Children working in mills were tasked with unskilled but often dangerous jobs. They had to clean the machines by crawling underneath and wiping fluff off the wheels and spindles while the machinery moved. This was called *fettling*. They had to repair broken threads on the spinning machines, which was called *piecing*.

A census from the 1800s shows children aged 11 and 12 years old doing the following jobs:

- soap maker
- street seller selling matches or ribbons
- general or house servant
- errand boy or girl
- railway message boy
- apprentice carpenter
- boiler cleaner on a tug boat
- shop boy
- apprentice chair maker
- pushing coal trucks in the mines
- cleaning streets of horse dung

# Education

In wealthier families, boys were sent away to fee-paying boarding schools whilst girls were usually taught at home by governesses. But even these children could face cruel punishments such as beatings or being made to wear a dunce's cap. It was only in 1870 that laws made it compulsory for every child between the ages of five and ten to attend school.

*Ragged schools* provided destitute and orphaned children with a basic education in the mid-1800s. They were set up by charitable organisations to enable all children to learn how to read and write.

Rich children learned their alphabet with ABC books in their playroom or nursery with a governess.

Once they were able to read, they could enjoy books such as:

- *Treasure Island* by Robert Louis Stevenson
- *Black Beauty* by Anna Sewell
- *Alice's Adventures in Wonderland* by Lewis Carroll

# Toys and Games

While richer children played with toy soldiers and tea sets, poorer children often only had homemade dolls or balls made out of bundles of rags. Candles provided the only light in the home once it was dark, so children mainly played outside during daylight hours.

Everyday toys might be a hoop and a stick. Marbles, catch and hopscotch were also popular games played by children at the time.

An abridged extract from the *Oxford Illustrated Dictionary of 19th Century Language*.

## Consider

Imagine what it was like to go to work as a very young child. How would you feel at the end of a very long day, still not having much to eat or many toys to play with? Think of <u>three words</u> to describe how you would <u>feel</u>.

# Childhood in the 1800s — Question Set 1

**1** The text begins *The life of a poor child in the 1800s was a harsh one.* What does this mean?

Tick one box

Children who were poor didn't live for very long. ☐

Children who were poor had a tough time. ☐

Children who were poor had a good life. ☐

Children who were poor didn't go to school. ☐

**2** Find two types of jobs children as young as 4 years old would have done in the 1800s.

1. ......................................................................................

2. ......................................................................................

**3** What was the difference between the education of girls and boys from wealthier families?

..............................................................................................

..............................................................................................

> When you are asked to compare two things, you have to mention both things in your answer.

*Year 3 Targeted Reading* © Not to be photocopied

**4** Match the first half of the sentence on the left with the correct second half on the right.

|  |  |
|---|---|
| Fettling was when children had to | pushing coal trucks in the mines. |
| Girls from rich families were | play outside in the day time. |
| A census showed that some 11 and 12-year-old children were | get underneath a machine to wipe fluff off its wheels. |
| Children could only | mend the broken threads on the spinning machines. |
| Piecing was when children had to | taught at home by a governess. |

(Girls from rich families were — taught at home by a governess.)

> Don't guess — look back over the text to find some of the key words. Only match them up when you're <u>sure</u> they're right.

**5** The text says: *It was only in 1870 that laws made it compulsory for every child between the ages of five and ten to attend school.*
What does *compulsory* mean? Circle one answer.

It has to be done.     There is a choice.

> Take your time with questions like this. Think about the meaning of the whole sentence you're given.

**6** The punctuation marks used to show the jobs that 11 and 12 year olds were doing in the 1800s are called "bullet points".
Why do you think these have been used instead of full sentences?

✏️ ......................................................................................................

......................................................................................................

# Childhood in the 1800s — Question Set 2

**1** Which statement best summarises the text under the subheading *Children at Work*?

**Tick one box**

All children were miserable in the 1800s. ☐

Children had to work in mills. ☐

Poor children often had hard, dangerous jobs to do. ☐

> Don't just tick which of the statements is <u>true</u>. 'Summarising' means saying in a few words what something is about.

**2** Which job mentioned in the section *Children at Work* do you think would have been the most dangerous? Give a reason for your answer.

| Most dangerous job: | ................................................................ |
|---|---|
| Reason: | ................................................................<br>................................................................<br>................................................................ |

**3** Look at the statements below and decide whether they are about poor or rich children.

|  | Poor children | Rich children |
|---|---|---|
| Children had to work for twelve hours at a time. | ☐ | ☐ |
| Parents paid for the boys' education. | ☐ | ☐ |
| Girls were taught to read by a governess. | ☐ | ☐ |
| Children played with tea sets. | ☐ | ☐ |

**4** Look at the two pictures below. One shows <u>poor</u> children and one shows <u>rich</u> children. Explain how you know which shows which.

This picture shows .................... children.

...........................................................................................

...........................................................................................

...........................................................................................

This picture shows .................... children.

...........................................................................................

...........................................................................................

...........................................................................................

**5** Why do you think families had to use candles for light in the 1800s?

...........................................................................................

## Challenge

The text shows how great it was to be a poor child back in the 1800s!

Do you agree or disagree? Circle your answer, and give three pieces of evidence from the text to support your answer.

Agree          Disagree

Evidence:

1. ......................................................................................

2. ......................................................................................

3. ......................................................................................

© Not to be photocopied                    Year 3 Targeted Reading

# Text 8 — Adventure Story

## The Mystery of Wickworth Manor

Sometimes adventure stories have a mystery that the characters in the story have to solve. *The Mystery of Wickworth Manor* by Elen Caldecott is a story about a boy and a girl named Curtis and Paige who meet on school trip and together solve a mystery. Here, Curtis has just arrived at Wickworth Manor and has found a gloomy room at the top of the house.

Slowly, the dark shapes and shadows turned into objects: a bank of filing cabinets, spilling paper; chairs stacked haphazardly, their legs sticking out like broken twigs; a cupboard with a door missing, and, against one wall, an old bed.

It wasn't a bedroom, it was a room where people dumped the things they didn't need any more. Curtis smiled, without humour.

This would suit him fine.

He could stay here and hide and not have to speak to anyone or explain anything to strangers. He could stay here and eat the biscuits in his suitcase and drink rainwater. He could sleep for seven days and when Mum came to collect him he would tell her what a brilliant time he'd had and they could drive home again in silence.

Curtis kicked off his shoes and fell back on to the bed.

It made a horrible crunching sound.

Curtis pressed his fingertips to his eyelids. Had he really just broken an antique bed? He was pretty certain that he had.

He opened his eyes and rolled off. He'd better take a look at the damage.

Underneath the bed it was dark and cluttered with yet more junk: hatboxes, old shoes, even a broken doll. A plank of wood lolled down from the frame, its edge jagged with splinters. That must be what he'd heard snap.

Curtis reached under the bed gingerly and pressed up against the plank. It waggled like a broken bone. He stretched as far as he could; his shoulder ached with the effort. He tried to ease the wood back into place, but it wouldn't realign. Something was jamming it. With his fingers outstretched he could just about touch whatever it was in the way of the plank.

It felt rough - maybe some kind of fabric? It had a square edge, covered in heavy cloth; it felt like an elbow in a sling. He grabbed the edge and tugged. It came loose. A few sharp yanks pulled it away from the bed frame. He sat back on his heels and pulled it clear of the bed.

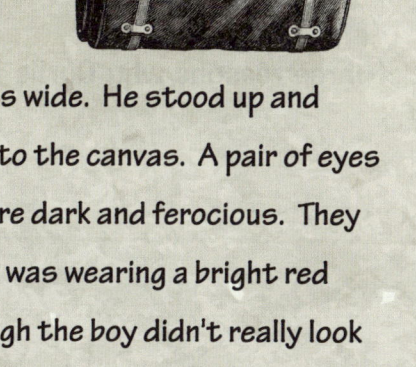

He unwrapped the cloth. And gasped.

It was a painting, about half a metre high and a bit less wide. He stood up and pulled the curtain a little until a puddle of light fell on to the canvas. A pair of eyes stared at him from inside the gilt frame. The eyes were dark and ferocious. They belonged to a boy with cropped hair and dark skin. He was wearing a bright red coat — some kind of servant's uniform, maybe? Though the boy didn't really look old enough to have a job; he looked about twelve or thirteen. The red coat had bright gold buttons, each one decorated with a map of the world, like tiny, gleaming globes. But it was the eyes that held Curtis's attention. Angry eyes, lost eyes, frightened eyes. Eyes that seemed to be looking at him as much as he was looking at them.

An extract from *The Mystery of Wickworth Manor* by Elen Caldecott.

## Consider

What do you think the mystery of Wickworth Manor could be that Curtis and Paige go on to solve? Use ideas and clues from the text extract to help answer this question.

# The Mystery of Wickworth Manor — Question Set 1

**1** Which of the following objects does Curtis see when he first enters the room?

**Tick all that apply**

paper ☐

broken twigs ☐

stacked chairs ☐

a bunkbed ☐

a cupboard with one door ☐

> It's really important to read the whole sentence to find the answers, not just individual words.

**2** List three reasons why Curtis thinks this room will *suit him fine*.

1. ....................................................................................

2. ....................................................................................

3. ....................................................................................

**3** a) What made Curtis look under the bed?

....................................................................................

....................................................................................

b) Find and copy the phrase in the story which shows that he decides to check under the bed.

....................................................................................

Year 3 Targeted Reading © Not to be photocopied

**4** *Curtis reached under the bed gingerly.* Which of the following words is most similar in meaning to the word 'gingerly'?

**Tick one box**

carefully ☐

excitedly ☐

quickly ☐

carelessly ☐

> If you don't know what the word means, try putting yourself in Curtis's position. How would you reach under the bed?

**5** Use the description in the final paragraph of the text to match the noun on the left to the correct adjective on the right.

| buttons | short |
| eyes | decorated |
| hair | red |
| coat | dark |
| skin | ferocious |

(eyes — ferocious)

> Do the ones you're sure of first.

**6** Number these events in the order they happen in the text.

Curtis hears a loud crunching sound. ☐ 1

He discovers an old, framed painting. ☐

Curtis opens a curtain. ☐

He looks under the bed. ☐

He pulls out something covered in cloth. ☐

> Remember — <u>find</u> and <u>underline</u> the events in the text. <u>Number</u> them in the text, then <u>match</u> the events in the question to these numbers.

# The Mystery of Wickworth Manor — Question Set 2

**1** Why do you think Curtis smiled *without humour*?

Tick one box

He thinks the room is a good hiding place. ☐

He doesn't have a sense of humour. ☐

He finds the room funny. ☐

> To get into the mind of the character, read the first part of the text again carefully for clues.

**2** What evidence is there in the text that a child might have once lived at Wickworth Manor?

..................................................................................................

..................................................................................................

**3** Why do you think the author chose to use the words *a puddle of light fell on to the canvas*?

..................................................................................................

..................................................................................................

..................................................................................................

..................................................................................................

> This question is about the <u>effect</u> the author's choice of words has on the reader. Think what a puddle looks like. What does *fell on to* suggest?

Year 3 Targeted Reading © Not to be photocopied

**4** Find evidence from the text which shows that Curtis is brave and curious.

| Adjective | Evidence from the text |
|---|---|
| brave | .................................................................................... .................................................................................... |
| curious | .................................................................................... .................................................................................... |

For this question, you need to find evidence from the text to support your choices.

**5** Find two clues in the text that show the painting was quite important and possibly precious to its owner.

1. ....................................................................................................

2. ....................................................................................................

## Challenge

Mystery stories always make the reader want to read on! Choose two details about the boy in the painting which make you want to read on.

| Detail of the boy in the painting | Why this makes me want to read on |
|---|---|
| 1. .............................................. .............................................. | .............................................. .............................................. |
| 2. .............................................. .............................................. | .............................................. .............................................. |

# Text 9 — Children's Fiction

## Danny, the Champion of the World

Roald Dahl's stories, such as *Charlie and the Chocolate Factory* and *Matilda*, have entertained millions of readers and even been turned into films and musicals. This extract is taken from Roald Dahl's novel *Danny, the Champion of the World*, which tells the story of Danny and his dad who live together in a caravan on the edge of a wood. Here, Danny's dad hasn't come home at night and Danny is looking for him in the wood, but is frightened of being found by the gamekeepers who patrol there.

I cannot possibly describe to you what it felt like to be standing alone in the pitchy blackness of that silent wood in the small hours of the night. The sense of loneliness was overwhelming, the silence was as deep as death, and the only sounds were the ones I made myself. I tried to keep absolutely still for as long as possible to see if I could hear anything at all. I listened and listened. I held my breath and listened again. I had a queer feeling that the whole wood was listening with me, the trees and the bushes, the little animals hiding in the undergrowth and the birds roosting in the branches. All were listening. Even the silence was listening. Silence was listening to silence.

I switched on the torch. A brilliant beam of light reached out ahead of me like a long white arm. That was better. Now at any rate I could see where I was going. The keepers would also see. But I didn't care about the keepers any more. The only person I cared about was my father. I wanted him back.

I kept the torch on and went deeper into the wood.

'Dad!' I shouted. 'Dad! It's Danny! Are you there?'

I didn't know which direction I was going in. I just went on walking and calling out, walking and calling; and each time I called, I would stop and listen. But no answer came.

After a time, my voice began to go all trembly. I started to say silly things like, 'Oh Dad, please tell me where you are! Please answer me! Please, oh please ...' And I knew that if I wasn't careful, the sheer hopelessness of it all would get the better of me and I would simply give up and lie down under the trees.

'Are you there, Dad? Are you there?' I shouted. 'It's Danny!'

I stood still, listening, listening, listening, and in the silence that followed, I heard or thought I heard the faint, but oh so faint, sound of a human voice.

I froze and kept listening.

Yes, there it was again.

I ran towards the sound. 'Dad!' I shouted. 'It's Danny! Where are you?'

I stopped again and listened.

This time the answer came just loud enough for me to hear the words. 'I'm here!' the voice called out. 'Over here!'

It was him!

**An extract from *Danny, the Champion of the World* by Roald Dahl.**

## Consider

**When Danny eventually sees his dad, he is bound to be relieved but quite emotional too. What do you think they will say to each other? How will each of them react?**

# Danny, the Champion of the World — Question Set 1

**1** How do you know from the introduction that Roald Dahl's stories are really popular?

..................................................................................................

..................................................................................................

**2** What is Danny doing alone in the wood?

Tick one box

Danny is hunting for the gamekeepers. ☐

Danny is searching for his Dad. ☐

Danny is shooting pheasants. ☐

Danny is hiding from his Dad. ☐

> With these multiple choice questions, decide which ones you're sure it's *not* first.

Who?
What?
Where?
When?
Why?

**3** Find and copy two phrases from the text to show Danny is out late at night.

1. ..................................................................................................

2. ..................................................................................................

*Year 3 Targeted Reading* © Not to be photocopied

**4** *The sense of loneliness was overwhelming. Circle one of these words which could replace the word 'overwhelming' in this sentence.*

exciting    enormous    calming

Try saying the sentence with each of the words. Which one sounds right?

**5** *Name three things in the wood that Danny thinks are listening with him.*

1. ......................................................................................

2. ......................................................................................

3. ......................................................................................

**6** *Number the following events to show what order they happened in the story.*

Danny switched his torch on. ☐

Danny heard his father calling "I'm here!" ☐

Danny began to call and shout for his dad. ☐

Danny went outside to look for his dad. ☐

Remember — you need first to <u>find</u> the events in the text and <u>underline</u> them. Then <u>number</u> them in the text in the order they appear. Then <u>match</u> the events in the questions to your numbered events in the text.

# Danny, the Champion of the World — Question Set 2

**1)** The light from the torch is described using the phrase *'like a long white arm'*. What type of writing is this?

**Tick one box**

alliteration ☐

simile ☐

rhyme ☐

**2)** Why do you think the author repeats the words *listened* and *listening* so many times in this extract?

..................................................................................................

..................................................................................................

..................................................................................................

..................................................................................................

> When you are asked why the author has done something, think what makes **you** do the same thing in **your** writing.

**3)** Find and copy evidence from the text to show Danny nearly gives up hope of finding his dad while he is in the wood.

..................................................................................................

..................................................................................................

..................................................................................................

**4** Thinking about the fact that Danny found his dad in the wood, what do you think might have happened to Danny's dad to explain why he hasn't come home?

..................................................................................................

..................................................................................................

..................................................................................................

> With this type of question, you need to try to imagine what happened earlier in the story. There's no 'right' answer — your answer just has to be believable.

**5** Give two pieces of evidence from the text which show that Danny cares about his dad.

1. ..............................................................................................

2. ..............................................................................................

> To help find the right evidence, think about how you might act if someone you cared about was in trouble.

## Challenge

> It's a good job Danny was so confident searching for his dad in the darkness and knew where he was going in the woods! He wouldn't have found his dad otherwise.

Explain why the cat is wrong about Danny. How did Danny actually find his dad in the end?

..................................................................................................

..................................................................................................

..................................................................................................

..................................................................................................

# Answers

## Text 1 — Poetry

### Pages 6 and 7: Poems About Trees — Question Set 1

1. You should have matched these pairs:
   willow — yellow
   birch — silver
   beech — brown
2. You should have ticked: dainty and sturdy
3. You should have mentioned any four of the following:
   elm, (English) oak, chestnut, lilac, poplar, plane
4. To the woodlands.
5. a) white
   b) 'Wearing white for Eastertide.' OR 'To see the cherry hung with snow.'
6. Edith Nesbit's favourite tree is **the plane tree**.
   The poem '**Loveliest of trees**' is about one tree.
   The tree that makes the churchyard shady is the **elm tree**.
   **A.E. Housman** thinks he will live for 70 years.

### Pages 8 and 9: Poems About Trees — Question Set 2

1. Example:
   She is saying that the leaves are glossy / shiny / look like a dress / look like material.
2. The table should be filled in like this:

   | Rhyming pattern: | Name of the poem it is used in: |
   | --- | --- |
   | AABB | Loveliest of trees |
   | ABAB | Child's Song in Spring |

3. You should have ticked: 20
4. Example:
   The city is where plane trees are mostly found, so they brighten the city / make the city a better place.
5. a) You should have ticked: The silver birch is a dainty lady. AND The willow is smart in a suit of yellow. AND The English oak is a sturdy fellow.
   b) 'Wearing white' OR 'the cherry hung with snow'

Challenge
   Your answer should mention that the blossom on the tree is so white that he compares it to snow.
   You could also have mentioned that the snow is a metaphor used to describe the blossom.

## Text 2 — Report

### Pages 12 and 13: Small School, Big Changes — Question Set 1

1. Because it is too small.
2. You should have ticked: He wanted to set up the first school.
3. You should have matched these names with these descriptions:
   Shahid Rajaei — The name of the first school in Kalou.
   Hamideh — A student of the school in Kalou.
   Kalou — A tiny fishing village in Iran.
   Abdul-Muhammad She'rani — The teacher who changed the lives of children in Kalou.
4. Any one of the following phrases:
   'it caught the attention of people all over the world.'
   'Kalou had gone from having no school to having one of the most famous schools in the world.'
5. Any two of the following items: money, books, letters, new desks, computer
6. You should have ticked: It is about a girl whose father changes his mind about her education.

### Pages 14 and 15: Small School, Big Changes — Question Set 2

1. Any one of the following reasons:
   Kalou can't be seen from satellite maps but now people know about it. OR Shahid Rajaei is now known for being the smallest school which is as good as being on the map. OR Kalou has now become famous but before people didn't even know the village existed.
2. There are lots of possible answers to this question.
   Example:
   I think he must have felt excited/grateful/relieved/proud because he really wanted the school to do well and he and the children had already worked hard to get it started.
3. Example:
   When the school became famous, he realised it was important for her to carry on at school.
4. The text says that in the teacher's blog he 'described the students' enthusiasm'.
5. a) You should have ticked: shocked
   b) Any suitable explanation. Example:
   I think she wants you to feel shocked because it will make you realise how lucky you are to go to school. It also might prompt people to do something about it and send gifts or money to small schools like this one in Iran.

# Answers

Challenge
    Example:
    I disagree. I think the girls' lives were changed more than the boys' because the text says 'life changed almost overnight for kids in Kalou, especially the girls.' This is because Shahid Rajaei showed how valuable education is, which convinced the government to make the bus route to the secondary school. The bus route means that girls like Hamideh can continue to go to school after Shahid Rajaei.

## Text 3 — Story in an Everyday Setting

### Pages 18 and 19: The Viking Warrior — Question Set 1

1. three years (ever since he started in Reception)
2. The children in Tristan's class do not like him. — true
   Tristan lives with his mum and dad. — false
   Tristan has a cousin called Jenny. — false
   Tristan likes playing with cars. — true
3. Any two of the following reasons:
   he wouldn't have to get up early for school, he wouldn't have to wear the uniform, he could go on fun trips
4. You should have matched these pairs:
   detested — hated
   snapped — said angrily
   droning — speaking boringly
   swivelled — turned around
5. a) the black sky
   b) echo
6. His dad named him after a racing driver.

### Pages 20 and 21: The Viking Warrior — Question Set 2

1. Any two of the following phrases:
   'This had not endeared him to the... children', 'other children avoid him', 'when alone on the playground', 'Unused to anyone talking to him'
2. Example:
   'Simmering' means 'ready to boil'. Anger is bubbling inside him, like water in a pot.
3. You should have ticked: because she says they will be learning about Vikings
4. Your answer may include these points:
   because he is often angry, because he's not friendly, because he might not be a good role model
5. a) You can choose either yes or no provided that you can give a reason to support your choice in part b).
   b) If you circled yes in part a), your answer could refer to the following:
   (*Both liking the Vikings*) They will become friends because they both like the Vikings so they can play together pretending to be warriors.
   (*Both not liking the teacher very much*) Ayrton describes the teacher as 'bossy' and Tristan thinks she drones on.
   (*Tristan seems happy that he has met Ayrton*) Tristan calls him his 'new-found friend' and thinks school might be better now.
   (*Ayrton is named after a racing driver*) Tristan likes Formula One cars so he might like Ayrton because he's named after a racing driver.

Challenge
    There is no evidence to suggest you should agree, so you should disagree. Example:
    I disagree because all the way through it talks about him not being popular with the teachers or with the children. He doesn't like the uniform and he asks his mum to be home-schooled. The first sentence of the text even says 'Tristan had never liked school'.

# Answers

## Text 4 — Myth

### Pages 24 and 25: Orpheus and Euridice — Question Set 1

1. He has three heads.
2. You should have ticked: She gave him confidence.
3. Thinking of Euridice calmed him down (and then he got an idea).
4. powerless
5. You should have matched these pairs:
   Hades — god of death
   Orpheus — musician
   Euridice — wife of Orpheus
   Cerberus — three-headed dog
6. You should have ordered the events like this:
   Orpheus knows Euridice is walking behind him. — 3
   Orpheus loses faith and goes back on his promise. — 4
   Orpheus walks away from the underworld. — 2

### Pages 26 and 27: Orpheus and Euridice — Question Set 2

1. You should have ticked: himself
2. Any two from:
   He said 'Beautiful! Very well done'.
   He 'clapped his hands'.
   He said 'your music impressed me'.
3. You should have ticked: frowned AND grumbled
4. Example: He is worried / anxious / concerned.
5. a) gasped
   b) Examples:
      How Euridice must feel: let down / angry / upset
      Why I think this: Orpheus had not trusted her to follow him.
      OR How Euridice must feel: Frightened
      Why I think this: She has to go back to the underworld.

Challenge

Your answer could have mentioned any of the following:
- Hades was testing Orpheus.
- Hades was seeing what kind of person Orpheus was.
- Hades was testing whether Orpheus trusted Euridice.

## Text 5 — Instruction Text

### Pages 30 and 31: Build Your Own Solar System — Question Set 1

1. To help the reader understand how big the solar system is.
2. Sun — washing machine
   Venus — pea
   Asteroid Belt — sand
   Mars — ball bearing
   Moon — pinhead
3. Mercury and **Mars** — **both ball bearings**
   Venus and **Earth** — **both peas**
   Uranus and **Neptune** — **both golf balls**
4. You should have given the planets the following numbers:
   Jupiter — 4, Venus — 2, Uranus — 5, Earth — 3
5. You should have circled: similar to
6. scale

### Pages 32 and 33: Build Your Own Solar System — Question Set 2

1. a) no
   b) *Reason*: Most people will not have the space to make the model. OR People will not want to ruin their washing machine, which they would do if they paint it yellow like the text says.
   *Evidence*: 'Here's the bad news – you are going to need a room about 2 km long!' OR 'Paint the washing machine yellow'.
2. People who understand scale and scientists who send rockets into space.
3. To show what a long distance it is OR Because Britain and Australia are on opposite sides of the world
4. Because people don't have rooms that are 2 km long
5. You should have ticked: a metre stick

Challenge

*Problems*: the planets will all be the same size, the bedroom won't be big enough.
*Reason*: The model the robot ends up with won't be a scale model of the Solar System, so it won't be as good as the model described in the text.

# Answers

## Text 6 — Playscript

### Pages 36 and 37: Alice in Wonderland — Question Set 1

1. At her new school (or boring-school)
2. You should have ticked: stranger
3. You should have made these sentences:
   Alice thinks she is **early**.
   White Rabbit thinks he is **late**.
4. You should have matched these examples with their descriptions:
   stage direction — 'A strange gate appears and opens.'
   OR 'The WHITE RABBIT runs through.'
   name of character speaking — 'ALICE:'
   what the character says — 'Curiouser and curiouser… It must be – it must be *tomorrow*, this must be boring-school! But it's really not *that* boring…'
5. Alice's mummy said she should make a good first impression. — true
   White Rabbit arrived on a train. — false
   The flowers are wearing colourful uniforms. — false
   Alice knows she is in Wonderland. — false
6. You should have given the events the following numbers:
   White Rabbit continues on his journey to meet the Queen. — 3
   The flowers laugh at Alice's lack of uniform. — 4
   Alice tells White Rabbit that she is a new girl. — 2

### Pages 38 and 39: Alice in Wonderland — Question Set 2

1. He is late for the Queen.
2. You should have ticked: bravo, convincing
3. a) You should have circled: confused
   b) Any two of the following examples:
      Curiouser and curiouser
      Pardon? I don't understand
      The *Queen* goes to this school?
      Was that yesterday?
      I — don't remember travelling here
4. Any two of the following examples:
   Oh dear, oh dear, I shall be late, I shall be late!
   No time, no time! Oh my ears and whiskers
   But the Queen, the Queen, I'm keeping her waiting!
   How late it's getting, how late!
5. You should have circled: unfriendly
   Example: They make fun of her for not having her uniform. They say 'Ha, look at *her*', which sounds like they are picking on her.

Challenge:
   Any two of the following pieces of evidence:
   'it must be *tomorrow*'
   'You can't be early when it's late!'
   'I came early, to make a good impression.' — 'A good impression of what?'
   'If she had the right look she would look just right.'
   'If she was like one of us she'd be just like one of us!'

## Text 7 — Non-Chronological Report

### Pages 42 and 43: Childhood in the 1800s — Question Set 1

1. You should have ticked: Children who were poor had a tough time.
2. Any two of the following answers: road sweeping, chimney sweeping, working down mines, working in factories, working in mills, fettling, piecing
3. Boys were sent away to boarding schools but girls were taught at home.
4. You should have matched these pairs:
   Fettling was when children had to — get underneath a machine to wipe fluff off its wheels.
   A census showed that some 11 and 12-year-old children were — pushing coal trucks in the mines.
   Children could only — play outside in the day time.
   Piecing was when children had to — mend the broken threads on the spinning machines.
5. You should have circled: It has to be done.
6. Examples:
   To make it easier to read OR to show it as a list

### Pages 44 and 45: Childhood in the 1800s — Question Set 2

1. You should have ticked: Poor children often had hard, dangerous jobs to do.
2. You could have picked any of the jobs mentioned in the text provided you could support your choice with a reason. Example:
   *Most dangerous job*: fettling
   *Reason*: Children were 'crawling underneath' the machinery and they were working 'while the machinery moved'. This made their job very dangerous because they could easily be hurt by the moving machinery.
3. Children had to work for twelve hours at a time. — poor
   Parents paid for the boys' education. — rich
   Girls were taught to read by a governess. — rich
   Children played with tea sets. — rich
4. The top picture shows **poor** children.
   Explanation: The children have ragged clothes and some aren't wearing shoes. They are standing around outside and have no toys to play with.
   The bottom picture shows **rich** children.
   Explanation: The children have smart clothes. They are in a lovely room and have toys to play with.
5. They did not have electricity in their homes.

Challenge
   You should have circled: Disagree
   You could have given any three pieces of evidence from the text that support your answer. Example:
   'Children as young as four years old worked 12-hour shifts in factories and mills',
   'Children working in mills were tasked with unskilled but often dangerous jobs',
   'poorer children often only had homemade dolls or balls made out of bundles of rags'

# Answers

## Text 8 — Adventure Story

### Pages 48 and 49: The Mystery of Wickworth Manor — Question Set 1

1. You should have ticked: paper, stacked chairs, a cupboard with one door

2. Any three of the following reasons:
   he can stay here and hide, he can sleep here, he can eat and drink here, he won't have to speak to anyone here, he won't need to explain anything to strangers

3. a) He heard a crunching sound and thought he might have broken the bed so decided to find out by looking under it.

   b) 'He'd better take a look at the damage.'

4. You should have ticked: carefully

5. You should have matched these words:
   buttons — decorated
   hair — short
   coat — red
   skin — dark

6. You should have given the events the following numbers:
   He discovers an old, framed painting. — 4
   Curtis opens a curtain. — 5
   He looks under the bed. — 2
   He pulls out something covered in cloth. — 3

### Pages 50 and 51: The Mystery of Wickworth Manor — Question Set 2

1. You should have ticked:
   He thinks the room is a good hiding place.

2. Example:
   Underneath the bed there is a 'broken doll'.
   OR The painting might be of a boy who lived at the manor.

3. Example:
   The word 'puddle' describes the shape of the patch of light — small and round. The word 'fell' shows how quickly the light came down when the curtains were opened.

4. 
   | Adjective | Evidence from the text |
   |---|---|
   | brave | He's alone in a house with 'dark shapes and shadows' and he doesn't mind. |
   | curious | He decides 'He'd better take a look' at what's under the bed. |

5. Any two of the following: it had a gilt frame, it was covered in cloth, it was quite a large painting

Challenge
   Examples:
   He was wearing something that looked like a 'servant's uniform' — I want to find out whether he had some kind of job.
   He had 'Angry eyes, lost eyes, frightened eyes' — I want to find out why he was angry, lost and frightened.
   The buttons were decorated with a 'map of the world' — I want to find out whether he had been travelling round the world.

# Answers

## Text 9 — Children's Fiction

### Pages 54 and 55: Danny, the Champion of the World — Question Set 1

1. They have entertained millions of readers OR some have been turned into films and musicals.
2. You should have ticked: Danny is searching for his dad.
3. the pitchy blackness, the small hours of the night, I switched on the torch
4. You should have circled: enormous
5. Any three of the following: the whole wood, trees, bushes, little animals, birds, the silence
6. You should have given the events the following numbers:
   Danny switched his torch on. — 2
   Danny heard his father calling "I'm here!" — 4
   Danny began to call and shout for his dad. — 3
   Danny went outside to look for his dad. — 1

### Pages 56 and 57: Danny, the Champion of the World — Question Set 2

1. simile
2. Example:
   The words 'listening' and 'listened' are repeated to show how quiet Danny has to be to try to hear his dad and how long he has to listen for. Danny feels like the animals, trees and even the silence are listening. This shows how incredibly quiet it is in the wood.
3. Any one of the following pieces of evidence:
   'the sheer hopelessness of it all' OR 'it all would get the better of me' OR 'I would simply give up and lie down under the trees'.
4. Any reasonable answer. Examples:
   Danny's dad could have fallen and hurt himself.
   Danny's dad might have been captured by the gamekeepers.
5. Any two of the following:
   The text says 'The only person I cared about was my father.'
   The text says 'I wanted him back.'
   Danny kept going even when he became scared.
   'It was him!' shows how relieved he was to hear his voice.
   Danny was pleading for his dad to tell him where he was.

Challenge

Example: We know Danny did not feel confident because the text says 'The sense of loneliness was overwhelming'. It also says that he didn't 'know which direction' he was going in as he ventured deeper into the wood. Then his voice begins to go trembly which shows his fear and he nearly gives up hope. He doesn't give up though and this helps him to find his dad — he has to keep persevering and keep listening.

---

## Acknowledgements

p.10-11: Excerpted from My School, Our World: Incredible and Unusual Schools Around the World, published by The Watts Publishing Group Limited (on behalf of Franklin Watts, A division of Hachette Children's Books) in the UK, used by permission of Owlkids Books, Toronto. Text © 2011 and 2016 by Susan Hughes. Image courtesy of Abdul-Muhammad Sherani.

p.16-17: The Viking Warrior by Maxine Petrie

p.22-23: Orpheus & Euridice by Duncan Lindsay

p.28-29: Copyright © Kjartan Poskitt, 1997. Reproduced with the permission of Scholastic Ltd. All rights reserved.

p.28: Solar System graphic © ANDRZEJ WOJCICKI/Science Photo Library/Getty Images

p.34-35: Alice in Wonderland © Glyn Maxwell, 2017 by kind permission of Oberon Books Ltd.

p.40-41: Abridged extract from Oxford Illustrated Dictionary of 19th Century Language by Oxford Dictionaries. Copyright © Oxford University Press 2018. Reproduced with permission of the Licensor through PLSclear.

p.41: Governess illustration © Universal History Archive/Universal Images Group/Getty Images

p.41: Hooping children illustration © German Scrap/Mary Evans Picture Library

p.46-47: © Elen Caldecott 2012, The Mystery of Wickworth Manor, Bloomsbury Publishing Plc.

p.52-53: Danny, the Champion of the World by Roald Dahl. Jonathan Cape Ltd and Penguin Books Ltd. © The Roald Dahl Story Company Limited, 1975.

Pages 3 and 64 contain public sector information licensed under the Open Government Licence v3.0.
http://www.nationalarchives.gov.uk/doc/open-government-licence/version/3/

Images & Clipart throughout the book from Corel ® and Clipart.com

# National Curriculum Content Areas

*Use the table below to record how pupils are doing in each of the National Curriculum Content Areas.*

## National Curriculum Content Areas

| | | 2a Word Meaning | 2b Retrieval | 2c Summarising | 2d Inference | 2e Prediction | 2f Text Meaning | 2g Language | 2h Comparison |
|---|---|---|---|---|---|---|---|---|---|
| Text 1: Poems about Trees | Set 1 | Q2 | Q4 Q6 | Q3 Q4 Q5a Q5b | | | Q1 Q5a Q5b | Q5a Q5b | Q2 |
| | Set 2 | | | | | | | | |
| Text 2: Small School, Big Changes | Set 1 | | Q2 Q3 Q4 Q5 | | Q2 Q4 | Q1 | | Q3 | |
| | Set 2 | | | | | | | | |
| Text 3: The Viking Warrior | Set 1 | Q4 | Q1 Q2 Q3 Q6 | Q1 | Q4 Q5 Q5b | | Q6 | Q2 | |
| | Set 2 | Q5b | Q3 | Q3 | | | | Q3 Q5a | |
| Text 4: Orpheus and Euridice | Set 1 | Q4 | Q1 Q5 | Q4 | Q1 Q2 Q4 Q5b | Q5 | | Q3 Q5a | |
| | Set 2 | | | | | | | | |
| Text 5: Solar System | Set 1 | Q5 Q6 | Q1 Q2 | Q4 | Q1 Q4 Q5 | | | Q3 | Q3 |
| | Set 2 | | | | | | | | |
| Text 6: Alice in Wonderland | Set 1 | Q2 | Q1 Q3 Q5 | Q3a Q6 | Q1 Q4 Q5 | Q4 | | Q2 Q3b | |
| | Set 2 | | | | | | Q6 | | |
| Text 7: Childhood in the 1800s | Set 1 | Q1 Q5 | Q2 Q4 | Q1 | Q2 Q4 Q5 | | | | Q3 |
| | Set 2 | | | | | | | | |
| Text 8: The Mystery of Wickworth Manor | Set 1 | Q4 Q5 | Q1 Q2 Q3a Q3b | Q6 | Q1 Q2 Q5 | | Q4 Q6 | | |
| | Set 2 | | | | | | Q6 | | |
| Text 9: Danny, the Champion of the World | Set 1 | Q4 | Q1 Q2 Q5 | | Q3 Q5 Q6 | | | Q2 | |
| | Set 2 | Q1 | | | | | | | |
| Total | | | | | | | | | |

E3RQ21